ALL CATS ARE ON THE
AUTISM
SPECTRUM

KATHY HOOPMANN

Foreword by Haley Moss

Jessica Kingsley Publishers
London and Philadelphia

Foreword

Haley Moss, Esq., autistic attorney, author, artist and advocate

Me-wow! I was 13 years old when my mom brought *All Cats Have Asperger Syndrome* home from an autism conference. You'd expect teenagers to think they're too old for picture books when they so desperately want to be seen as adults, but nope – the adorable cats and simple yet positive words to connect everything together made me, a lifelong dog owner and lover, feel a deep connection with cats and autism. I couldn't describe the magic of how cats perfectly explained everything I felt and knew about myself. Kathy's stunning depictions of autism resonated deeply with me. I was already confident and proud to be autistic, and that pride was solidified in a picture book.

Smiles from the book's feline friends were contagious within my house; my mom and dad shared the magic of cats on the autism spectrum with me. I couldn't stop thinking about the many ways *All Cats Have Asperger Syndrome* made me smile as an autistic teenager, and the book loyally sits in my joy-filled autism library well into adulthood.

I unabashedly say this is one of my favorite books of all time. In the twelve years I've had my copy of *All Cats*, it has been a trusty sidekick and teaching tool. Friends and strangers alike have all felt the heartwarming effect of this book and a shared connection to me whenever I introduced them to it. It's the book I used to tell my high school best friend I was autistic. It's the book I kept on my desk at my law office to make colleagues, clients, and visitors feel comfortable learning about autism. It's a book that reminds me that being different is not a bad thing and, sometimes, people on the autism spectrum are both celebrated and misunderstood just like our feline companions.

Cats on and off the page can change hearts and minds. I never had a cat in my life outside of this book until a little over a year ago, but now, I see myself in her. I see my cat in me with our autistic traits, and I can now say all cats are definitely on the autism spectrum.

When Kathy mentioned that my all-time favorite autism book was getting an update to be more inclusive of people all across the spectrum (including us girls!), I was thrilled. When I told my parents that I was fortunate enough to have the honor of writing a foreword to one of my favorite books in the world, my mom freaked out, remembering this was the book that caught her eye so many years back and that continues to touch our hearts.

All Cats Are on the Autism Spectrum is like receiving a hug from a lifelong friend you haven't seen in a while. You will always be close with an indescribable bond. Knowing future generations of young people on the spectrum and their families will get to enjoy this book for years to come makes me think we will have a more understanding, accepting generation of cat lovers who become better friends to autistic children and adults alike.

May this book fill your day with meows, laughs, play, smiles – and some new friends and understanding during your journey. Your mileage may vary, but I am still delightfully sharing and spreading the magic of *All Cats Are on the Autism Spectrum* – and hope you do, too.

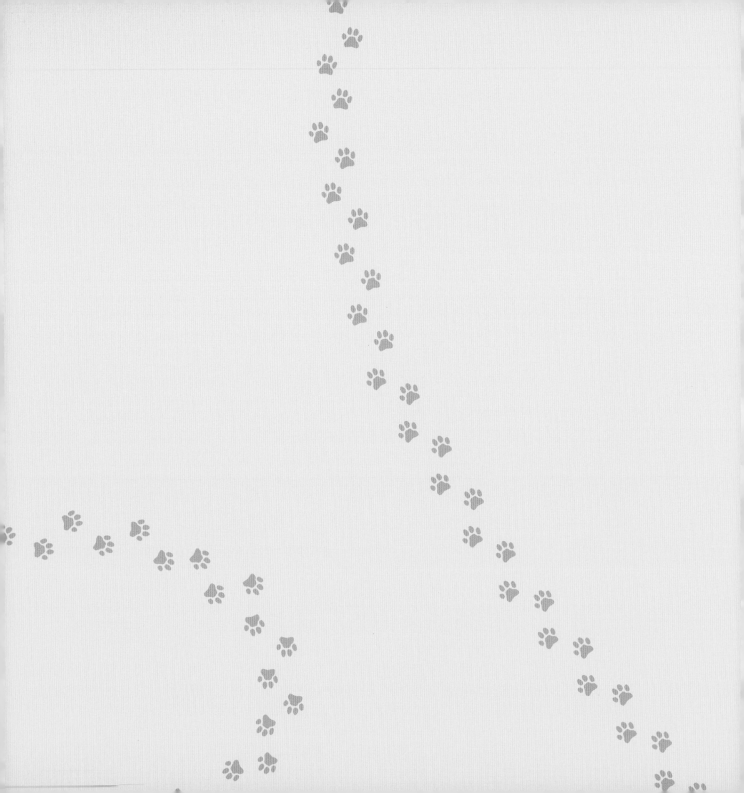

A Note from the Author

What's in a name? A lot actually.

In 2006, I wrote *All Cats Have Asperger Syndrome* with the express purpose to demystify the diagnosis in a fun, easy-to-read format. In 2013, the diagnostic tool used by professionals in the United States (the DSM-5) eliminated the term *Asperger Syndrome* and placed it under the generic umbrella of *Autism Spectrum Disorder*. *Asperger Syndrome* was now to be diagnosed as *Autism Spectrum Disorder (ASD) Level 1*. Now that's a mouthful!

Since then, there has been much debate and confusion about the correct terminology to be used. Is it Autism Spectrum Disorder (ASD) or Autism Spectrum Condition (ASC) or just the Autism Spectrum (AS)? Should we say *a person with autism* or *an autistic person* or *someone who is neurodiverse*?

Apart from the change in the diagnostic terms used, other changes were occurring in the autism community. In 2006, it was generally accepted that most of those diagnosed were boys. Now it is known that many girls are on the spectrum. As *All Cats Have Asperger Syndrome* was written with male pronouns, this needed addressing.

Fifteen years ago it was considered empathetic to say there is a little bit of Asperger's in us all. Now that statement is recognised as not only incorrect but insulting to those on the spectrum as it belittles the very real challenges they face daily.

So when it came time to update my book to current terminology and sensitivities, I was faced with a very difficult task to get things right, especially knowing that word usage and correctness changes regularly.

All Cats Are on the Autism Spectrum is written with the very best intentions to reflect the wishes of the autistic community in language and concepts. I know that my choices will not please everyone and that views on language will continue to evolve. However, words do matter, and sometimes we get things wrong, and that's ok if we are gracious about respecting the views of others and are prepared to use their preferred language once we know what it is.

I pray that my readers will see past the finer details of disagreement and join with me in celebrating, and deepening our understanding of, the richness and diversity of the autistic community.

The first signs of autism are usually
picked up very young.

Those on the spectrum look at the world in their own unique way.

They like to be near those they love,
but might not want to be held,

preferring squishy places to a hug.

Instead of coming to people for comfort,
they may prefer a toy or a pet.

They can be extra adventurous,

and use up some of their nine lives all too quickly.

Autistic people often have exceptionally good hearing, and loud sounds and sudden movements may scare them.

Yet at times they don't respond to their name
or requests as if they can't hear at all.

Their other senses can be
heightened too, such as touch

"I hate
bath days!"

"Are you wearing perfume?"

and smell.

They are often fussy about what they eat,

and may want the same food presented
in the same way, day after day.

13

"A morning nap on *my* chair."

Daily rituals comfort them,

and they get worried if their schedules
or surroundings are changed.

"Dinner is 2.42 minutes late!"

Yet they may find it hard to stay organised
and manage their own time.

Autistic people aren't all the same though,
and their strengths and challenges are like tangles
of colour, each a little different from the next.

Their abilities and preferences are not fixed,

Good at
maths

Only eats
white food

Doesn't like
to be touched

Hates
change

Loves
trains

18

and can change from hour to hour, day to day,
depending on moods, foods, and even the weather.

Their faces don't always show
how they are feeling inside,

and people may think they have no emotions, which is not true at all.

"This *is* my happy face!"

Crowds confuse them and they are not sure how to behave.

They can find body language difficult to read,

"Are you my friend?"

23

and may upset others without knowing why,

which keeps them awake at night, wondering what they did wrong and what they could have done differently.

Others follow fads

that might
not interest
those on the
spectrum at all.

If they do want to fit in, they may pretend to be something they are not, which is exhausting, and can't be kept up for long.

When life gets too much for them,
they might have a meltdown,

30

which they don't do on purpose, can't control
and feel terrible about afterwards.

They may become loners caught up in a world of their own,

where they can do their own
thing over and over again

without being
disturbed.

"I love ailurophiles!"

Autistic people may have a very advanced vocabulary,

but then they get little words all mixed up

"I hope this tree
doesn't bark!"

or misunderstand what people say.

"I haven't let the
cat out of the bag!"

When they are spoken to, they may refuse to make eye contact.

"I like to sleep in boxes, in baskets, on beds, in bowls..."

When *they* talk, they go on and on about the same topic
or ask the same questions over and over again

and don't pick up clues that those
around them are bored silly.

Although their families don't always understand the things they do, they love them all the same and can become very protective.

In many ways, those on the spectrum
think more deeply than their peers.

"Catnip tastes great and it also repels mosquitos!"

They may know fascinating facts about their special interests,

or have amazing memories,

"We bought this cactus 215 days ago."

45

or go to great
lengths to test their
latest theories,

"See! The moon *is*
bigger up here."

and people marvel at their bright intelligent minds.

Often they have a great sense of humour, but they don't always realise that what they are saying

"You look silly wearing that!"

And they are honest, which is great of course, although
they might be more honest than some prefer.

50

"Milk? What milk?"

When they try to tell a lie, they are not very good at it.

They treat
everyone equally,
regardless of age,
size or authority,

and are not afraid to stand up for
what they believe to be right and fair.

However, as they grow older, they may feel different from everyone else, as if they belong on an alien planet,

like an outsider looking into a world
they never truly understand.

Yet, with their unique perspective on life,

their eye for details that others often miss,

and their passion for researching
something they love,

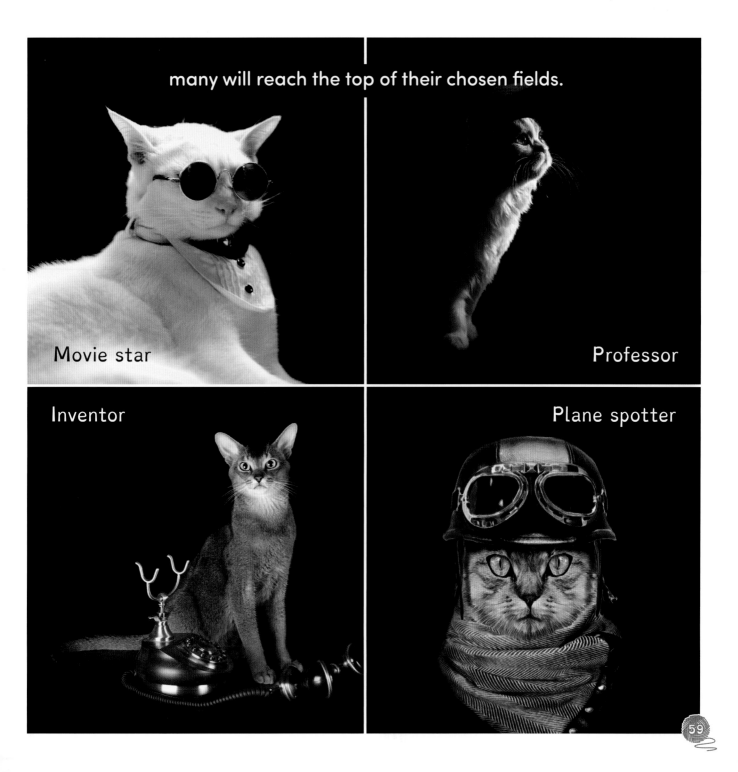

many will reach the top of their chosen fields.

Movie star

Professor

Inventor

Plane spotter

Sure, they may need
a little help following
fashionable trends,

but don't forget that *everyone* is important in the tapestry of life.

So those on the spectrum are just like everyone else.
They need love, encouragement and a purpose for life,

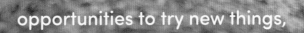
opportunities to try new things,

and space to be themselves,

and then everyone can sit back and enjoy the
unique individuals they become.

Cat names and photograph credits

Cover image
Ginger Cat © Seregraff

page 1
© Ilike

page 2
© Elena Mitusova

page 3
Siberian Cat © Lubava

page 4
© Koldunov Alexey

page 5
© Liliya Kulianionak

page 6
© Stephane Bidouze

page 7
© Andrey_Kuzmin

page 8
© Irina Kozorog

page 9
© Irina Kozorog

page 10
© atiger

---

page 11
Scottish Fold © Seregraff

page 12
Chinchilla Persian
© cynoclub

page 13
© WildlifeWorld

page 14
© dezy

page 15
© otsphoto

page 16
© Esin Deniz

page 17
© De Jongh Photography

page 18
© Felicia Williams

page 19
© Pi_Kei

page 20
Sphynx © Loginova Elena

page 21
Exotic Calico Shorthair
© Daisy Heart

---

page 22
© Khamidulin Sergey

page 23
British Shorthair
© Chendongshan

page 24
© GuponStudio

page 25
Siamese © Esin Deniz

page 26
© FotoYakov

page 27
© Katho Menden

page 28
Scottish Fold © Autobahn

page 29
© Africa Studio

page 30
Maine Coon © Cat'chy
Images

page 31
© ANASTASIIAKU

page 32
© Fotokostic

page 33
© Konstanttin

page 34
© osobystist

page 35
© Elizaveta Galitckaia

page 36
© Davaiphotography

page 37
© Koldunov Alexey

page 38
Scottish Fold © Wirestock Images

page 39
Maine Coon © Kachalkina Veronika

page 40
© liveostockimages

page 41
© Volodymyr Plysiuk

page 42
White British Cat © SunRay BRI Cattery RU

page 43
© Volodymyr Burdiak

page 44
© Photosite

page 45
Scottish Fold © Taras Demborynskyi

page 46
© Andrey Khusnutdinov

page 47
© Kseniia Kolesnikova

page 48
Maine Coon © Liliya Kulianionak

page 49
Sphynx © Seregraff

page 50
© Irina Kozorog

page 51
© SunRay BRI Cattery RU

page 52
© Sergey Petrov

page 53
© vvvita

page 54
© Sonsedska Yuliia

page 55
© Orhan Cam

page 56
Sphynx © Oleg Mikhaylov

page 57
© yadamons

page 58
© Tang Trung Kien

page 59
Abyssinian © Shchipkova Elena
© StudioLondon
© GrooveZ
Scottish Fold © Dmitrijs Mihejevs

page 60
© Hannamariah

page 61
© Eric Isselee

page 62
British Shorthair
© Chendongshan

page 63
© oleg kuzminov

page 64
© Chepko Danil Vitalevich

page 65
© Foonia

First published as "All Cats Have Asperger Syndrome" in 2006
by Jessica Kingsley Publishers
This revised edition published in Great Britain in 2021
by Jessica Kingsley Publishers
An Hachette Company

1

A CIP catalogue record for this title is available from the British
Library and the Library of Congress

ISBN 978 1 78775 471 3
eISBN 978 1 78775 472 0

Printed and bound in China by Leo Paper Products

Jessica Kingsley Publishers' policy is to use papers that are natural,
renewable and recyclable products and made from wood grown
in sustainable forests. The logging and manufacturing processes
are expected to conform to the environmental regulations of the
country of origin.

Jessica Kingsley Publishers
73 Collier Street
London N1 9BE, UK

www.jkp.com

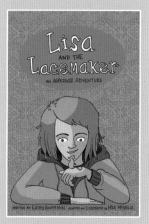

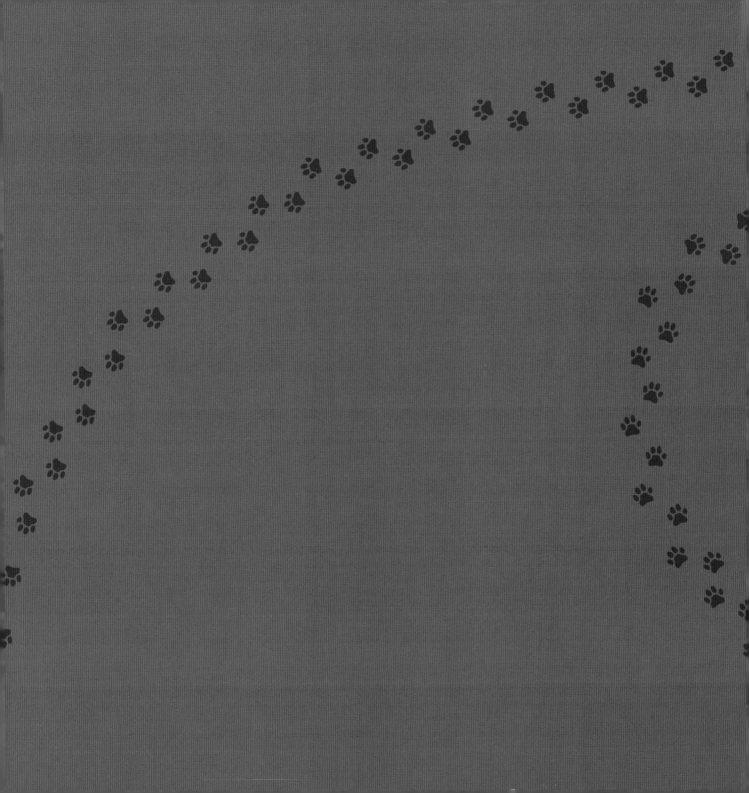